AF316779

This is dedicated to:

My Aunt Shirley, who passed in the pandemic. She always motivated me to push through my shyness because there was something great inside, and that was greatness.

You pushed me for my first speaking opportunity. Even when I kept saying no, you didn't give up on me, with me not realizing you were preparing me for so much more. This is for you Auntie. I know you would be proud. Love you. Miss you.

TABLE OF CONTENTS

INTRODUCTION

Hello, to all and to all, hello! So, a brief story on how this came about. It's not a lengthy story. On October 7, 2022 at 3:42 p.m., I was at my grandmother's house. I don't know what I was doing at that moment, but I remember God telling me to write a book on the season that I am in. I am in a season of feeling stuck. I have so many things I can envision myself doing to the extent that I don't know what to do.

For those who know me, they know I don't act based on what people think or say; I need to pray on it. Now, don't be confused.....I believe that we have free will. However, there are some things in my life that I just need God to instruct me on. For those of you who are chosen, then you can understand the frustration when you ask for help and you don't get an answer.

INTRODUCTION

For those who are confused, look at it like this: You ask your teacher to help you solve a problem, and the teacher hasn't answered your question. That's where I am. Right now.......Currently......Sadly.

But there is a bright side to every situation. Being in this predicament, I can help other purposeful people who feel the way I do on how to overcome this place that we feel is a drought. I really believe that this drought is about to connect to a well that never runs dry! Lastly, I hope and pray that this self-help book will motivate, inspire, and truly make a difference in your life. Let's jump in!

I'M
Stuck.

FRUSTRATION.

In this Waiting Season, I have been feeling a multitude of emotions: fear, discomfort, anxiety, sloth, curiosity, confidence, etc. This book itself is an affirmation, an opportunity for me to speak life unto myself and you! Let's go straight to work. The first you need to know is: **Everything is going to work out.** When you are in a season where you are confused, you can feel as if you're missing out on opportunities, you're behind schedule, you're not being heard, etc. I want to simply tell you that you're right on schedule. Sometimes, if you're an overthinker, like myself, then you must learn how to trust and depend on God, that everything is working in your favor and that you have no reason to fear.

Even when challenges arise, solutions will eventually unveil themselves, often in unexpected ways. Find solace in the knowledge that even in the darkest moments, there's a light at the end of the tunnel; every setback is an opportunity for growth and every failure a stepping stone towards success. So, with unwavering faith and perseverance, we navigate through life's storms, knowing that ultimately, everything is going to work out. Take deep breaths, affirm that you are purposeful, and that you are destined for greatness. Eventually, your creativeness will kick in to wonder and establish something that can be life-changing for you and your family!

What's for you is for you.

A lot of times, we try to make things work for us that are not good fits. Then, we get upset when things don't work out; but it's simply because that was never a part of our puzzle; we just tried to force some wrong pieces together. When God is involved, things align smoothly. In this process, there is no force required; everything flows. Sometimes, when we are the main ones involved, things don't go as planned. Even if it doesn't go as planned, it doesn't mean that you give up. Pray for guidance along your path as you move forward.

Take your losses as lessons.

How many times have you been in a situation that didn't go the way you envisioned, and you beat yourself up about it to the point where you felt lost? We must stop treating ourselves that way. Sometimes, we waste time by not learning the first time, but I'm not referring to that particular moment. However, there is a reason for everything we endure; we just must take the time to figure out the lesson. I'm currently going through a particular season, and I feel like I've been in the same situations, even though I kept my integrity and my peace. But right now, I'm taking a step back to analyze this season. I'm also leaning more on God to fight for me than I am leaning on myself to retaliate because throughout this difficult season, I'm learning endurance, patience, resistance, and so much more. There is always something to learn throughout this journey.

Don't let your breakdown breakup your destiny.

I know that during a season of waiting, you tend to break down, go into a depression, feel like you're never coming out, or want to give up, etc. BUT, you must remain hopeful. You must motivate yourself because, many times, we won't vocalize, we just internalize our emotions. Then when we internalize, the challenge maximizes. Once it maximizes, then eventually, if we're not careful, the destiny dies. So, you must keep reminding yourself that this will soon be over and until then, I will speak positively about myself and my future.

Wake up.

There will be times once you are towards the end of the season when you will feel that the moment that you're in will never end. You might feel hopeless and empty, and might even think this is going to be your life. WE must encourage ourselves, especially if you're like me, and you don't tell anyone how you feel. There will be times when you'll experience a certain kind of tiredness that will require you to motivate yourself to get out of the rut and press toward whatever God has in store for you. When some people wake up, they have what we call "sleep" on their eyes. Sleep is the crust (and sometimes goo) that can accumulate in your eyes during sleep. It's hard to get up once you wake up, so sleep does not help the situation. However, once you get the sleep out of your eye, you'll be able to move around better. Let me guess: You're trying to figure out this analogy/metaphor. It's simple: Sleep represents our fears. We're kind of asleep in that we feel that we are not moving; we're stuck. Our eyes represent the path that is clearly set for us. For us to wake up (fulfill our purpose), we must get the sleep (our fear) out of the way, so we can see (to move in the right direction). So, let's get the sleep out of our eyes and start doing something.

Ridicule vs. Reward

Sometimes we feel ridiculed for being in such a season, and to be honest, a lot of that ridicule comes from our own selves. If people around you try to ridicule you, especially without fully knowing the circumstances, then they don't need to be a person of interest when you are looking for someone to talk to. Now, nothing is wrong with constructive criticism, and there sure isn't anything wrong with being real with one another. I always tell my friends that if I'm wrong, please tell me. I do that because I don't need "yes men." I need people who will get on my tail even for the smallest things because I simply want to be the best version of myself.

However, that shouldn't always be the direction the conversation goes in; correction isn't even ridicule, anyway. Regarding ourselves, we must keep the faith and understand the reward of this period we are in. Once you look at the bigger picture, you won't be so hard on yourself to the point of disdain or ridicule.

Setbacks Aren't Always Setups.

Ok...ok...ok. You thought you were going to be so much farther along right now. You thought this, and you thought that. We, again, must take things into perspective. You ever thought ahead, like further past where your expectation was? For example, your expectation is a job promotion, but you've envisioned owning a business. Maybe you're not at the expectation point because you're supposed to exceed it. When you are supposed to surpass your vision, it's going to take additional time. In all honesty, for some of you, like myself, the visions I have take a lot of time already!

So, I know if what God has for me is better than what I think (which it is), then that could take even longer!!! Sometimes, your delay is just a deductible to get to your destiny...........................THAT. WAS. GOOD. TO. ME.

FIXATION.

Who are you listening to?

Being in a waiting season causes a shift. With that being said, everyone will not understand your shift. I have realized this so much, y'all, to the point where I literally cannot stress this enough. I've been listening to Myron Golden, Nehemiah Davis, Sean O'Connell, Milan Harris, and more. I watch them, view their masterclasses, and receive emails from them because they are at a place where I want to be, and they have been successful in an area that sparks my interest. I feel like it's pointless to watch someone just because they have a following. I need to be invested into who you are and what you do, and not who follows you. To be honest, I need to drown my ears with videos and audios from them. I watch it, but I don't watch it enough. In a season like this, you must be TREMENDOUSLY careful about what you allow yourself to hear.

Who are you listening to? (part 2)

Some people mean well; however, where you may be going is beyond their capacity, or mindset even. They can't go there. But they will try and deter you from accomplishing anything that is not what they are used to. If you limit what you share, the less their response will offend you. This does not apply to those of you who just want your way with no strategy, as if things will happen out of the air or something. No...no...and heck no. For example, I am in a beginning season of entrepreneurship. If I tried to explain some of my hardships to my grandmother, who comes from picking cotton and working for around a couple dollars per hour, it would be challenging because in her mind, you need "a good government job, so you can have benefits." My parents would tell me I need a "real job." I would often ask my parents, "What is a 'real job' to you?" If I make $17 an hour, that rounds to about $140 for 8 hours. Now for my fellow musicians, we can get $200-300 for a 2-hour service and have the rest of our day to ourselves. When you look at it, which do you think is better? I know that working five days a week on a 9-5 might yield more money overall or even include certain benefits, but a musician, entrepreneur or otherwise creative person can use their talents and skills to maximize

their earnings and overall potential
during the same time period with
greater, more satisfying results.

It. Is. Me.

I know some of you guys reading this had to doubled back to make sure you read what you read. Even though it may not be what we want to hear, it's what we need to hear! For some of us, WE ARE OUR OWN SETBACK! Whether it is allowing ourselves to overthink, to overcompensate, to give up and to give in to thoughts of negativity...that. is. US! Some lack accountability, so let me be one of the first, if not the first, to say that you're doing too much!!! Like, chill out. Take deep breaths because I know that was hard...if you're still reading this, congratulations, and welcome back!

Stop convincing yourself that you are not good enough and start telling yourself that you ARE. Stop telling yourself that you are what people say you are and start telling yourself what you know yourself to be! (Hopefully, what you know is accurate) Ok, enough jokes. On a serious note, keep aiming to break those generational barriers. Keep aiming to be a stable individual. Keep aiming to decrease those carbs. Whatever it is that you're aiming towards, regardless of where you are right now, remind yourself of what is to come! The more you remember how half-full the glass of water is, the more you'll forget how half empty the glass was!

Do what works for you.

I was the only one in my immediate family to study music, and one of the grandchildren to attend postsecondary school right after high school. So, the response was slightly different. I was asked to change my major several times or at least go with Music Education. Only a few of my extended cousins are successful in music. My mom has been a nurse for over 25 years. My grandmother and the majority of my aunts are nurses. My dad is a teacher and truck-driver. My grandfather and some of my uncles are military. You get my point lol! So their faith in an industry like that is very vague. Even when I quit my job and didn't truly have a backup, the response was exactly the same. You see, guys...working for 40-50 years making an average income surpassed what their parents had, so in their eyes, that should be the goal. For me, I'm supposed to exceed them, so the 9-5 for that long ain't it. Now, let's be clear: Every Gen Z or Millennial is not meant to be their own boss; so, please don't try it if it's not for you. For some people, that "real job" is perfectly fine! Me, personally, I have always been a misfit in a way, so I tend to do things out of the ordinary. Even when I stopped working, somehow, some way, I never lacked. I needed that time away to push me to become the best that I can be.

BE. QUIET.

I know it's hard, but sometimes, you have to shut up. Take whatever comes, but remain calm and remain silent. People want you to react; people want you to blow up; people want you to get out of character...Be Quiet. I know it is way harder than it sounds, but one thing about this season that I'm in, God has proven Himself to be with me the whole time. I mentioned what this season is helping me to improve on; each time, I get frustrated, I get mad, I want to address something; I want to spazz out; but I end up keeping quiet. God reveals something to me EVERYTIME. So, there is strength in what seems to be your weakness.

Listen.

Sometimes, we're the only ones talking and we forget to listen. It's important while you're in this season, to do less talking and more listening. And we can do that without allowing others' opinions to negatively affect us. Just listen. If you do speak, wait, so that what you say in response is the right thing to say. Listen, digest, pray, and move accordingly. And to be quite honest, some things aren't even worth speaking on. Some of us talk extensively with very little walking. By using the term "very little walking," I mean saying one thing without sticking to your word. I understand that I don't have to announce to others my footsteps; they just need to listen out for them.

P.R.A.Y.

Nothing long about this. We must pray consistently, without ceasing. Don't just pray to get out of this moment; continue to pray so that you can endure the next. Pray just to thank God for keeping you. I don't need to always have a Christmas list full of things. Sometimes, I just tell Him, "Thank you," and that's it. Sometimes, I just ask for guidance. The length of the prayer doesn't matter; He just needs you to trust Him and realize that what He wants is going to happen. I also pray to be in His will, not just mine. Keep in mind, life and death are really in your mouth. Therefore, words have the power to shape our thoughts, emotions, and actions. The language we use can influence our mindset and attitudes, as well as how we perceive life in this world. Positive and uplifting words can bring encouragement and inspiration, while negative and harmful words can lead to despair and destruction.

Limit your conversation.

Don't get it twisted. I love my family, but I come from a different era than many of them, a number of whom have never even attempted to do what I am doing. Thus, they can't relate because they feel like a "real job" is the only solution. Listen, I get it. It can be frustrating because if I talk about my struggles, I just need support to keep going. Holla' back if you feel me. I don't even want financial assistance; I just need motivation because it's my vision. Today, this is why I limit what I share to refrain from the potential frustration because I know their reaction isn't intended to discourage me. They are sincerely attempting to "help me" based on their current knowledge. To this day, I still respect their knowledge and wisdom.

FRUITION.

Keep Going.

I know how it feels to be in this stuck state, TRUST ME! That is why I'm writing because I realize it is one thing to talk about, but totally another thing to experience it personally. All of us, sometimes, must wait, whether it's waiting on our oil change, waiting for a relationship, waiting in the checkout line or even for some fire sneakers to drop. However, there's a difference between a waiting moment and a waiting season. For instance, there's a difference between waiting in traffic due to an accident and waiting at home for weeks due to snow. Whatever path your waiting is on, I just want you to remain determined to be the best, even when you don't know what your best contains. Vow to yourself to be consistent with your plans and goals, because if you aren't consistent, no one else will hold you accountable! Even if your waiting period is longer than you thought it would be, vow to do whatever is good that's in your heart. Every idea, every plan, every trip, every dream.......keep going!

No Repeats.

Whatever you received from this season, remember it! If this season taught you to endure, then when the next hardship comes (because it will), it shouldn't bother you like the last one did. I'm not saying you will be invincible, but what I am saying is to not be so easily moved. If you made it out of this just fine, then the slightest inconvenience or form of adversity should not set you back that far. In life, you can handle anything that comes your way. It wouldn't happen if you weren't capable yet. Again, don't be so deceived; you got this.

I am victorious.

Sometimes, being in a predicament where there's no control can make you consider that you're a loser, that this is a battle that has been lost, that you're a joke, and for me, way worse. Being stuck can put a person in a low place, emotionally and mentally. Other life situations can sometimes even add to what you're feeling. Regardless of what comes your way, remember that you are more than a conqueror, and that there is nothing that is thrown your way that you cannot handle!

Anything is possible.

Sometimes, we think things are so far-fetched, either because we're the first to do it or what we're doing is different than what we've known. Different can be difficult, it can also be deserving. That was good to me! Now, the different I'm referring to is Good Different. Bad Different is not only difficult, but it's also draining. Which brings me to the question: What difference do you bring? Ok, ok...that was a little moment for me. As you can see, I am also adding little side-pieces for myself that you might consider, so that you won't feel like you're alone. In my waiting season, I'm trying to do things that are different, which makes it difficult, but not too distant, that I can't do. Due to this, I have to constantly remind myself of the future that I am trying to create, the ways that I am trying to make, and the doors that I want God to open for me. Regardless of my lineage, regardless of my past, I know that I can do all things. So, just remember when you're beating yourself up, when you want to give up, when you feel like you're falling apart, You. Can. Do. Anything. Just play: "Impossible" (the Whitney Houston and Brandy version).

Havoc vs. Hope.

Whose report will you believe? The report of chaos or change? Suffering or Solace? Agony or Arrival? This season greatly relates to your perception. How we view things will play a crucial role in how we will move forward. In difficult situations, we sometimes focus more on the distraction than we do the discipline. We stress on being tested more than we rely on the text we learned from. The negativity of a circumstance already has most of our attention. People love speaking about the negative, especially in video footage, social media, and pillow talk. There's so much negative build-up to the point where your additional remarks will continue to keep yourself from growing. You do not need to be focusing on that; you must bring out the positive. Instead of gleaning on our catastrophes, we must garner our continuation.

Set Realistic Goals.

Ok, we are near the end, but I have to say this: Set goals for yourself! Everybody isn't the best at this (trust me cause I'm not lol), but it's how you look at it. Goal setting relies on a dynamic and adaptive approach, requiring periodic reflection and adjustment. A self-help journey involves not only the pursuit of goals but also the continuous evolution of those goals in tandem with personal growth. Goal setting, when approached with mindfulness and flexibility, transforms into a transformative tool that empowers individuals to sculpt the life they envision, infusing each step with intention and meaning.

Embrace the New!

Embracing change is a cornerstone of personal growth and self-discovery, an essential in a fulfilling life. In the realm of self-help, the ability to accept change is not a skill, but a mindset. Change happens either by circumstance or choice. I know...you don't like it, but that's only because it stems from a place called unfamiliarity. The hardest part is that the same place we fear can bring so much into our future. That place can cause pain, but it can also bring you purpose. The majority of change isn't bad and in fact, I look for change within my circle. When you finally embrace change, it can help you go through life's twist and turns with a sense of adaptability and fortitude. Once you embrace it, you would be so peaceful.

CONCLUSION

Now we are coming to an end, so let's recap what we went over. Regardless of how you feel, know that everything is going to work out. What's for you will always be for you. Always take your losses as lessons. Don't let your breakdown breakup your destiny. Wake up from whatever funk you're in! There's a difference between Ridicule and Reward. Setbacks aren't always Setups, so analyze the situation. Pay attention to who you're listening to and what they are saying. Sometimes, YOU are the problem. The key is to recognize it and change for the better. Make sure that you do what works for you and nobody else. Also, make sure what you're doing is indeed working. Remain silent during seasons such as this; you can't focus on preparing for what's to come if you keep talking about what is right now...which goes right along with listening. Pray always, not just for the material things, but mainly with thanksgiving for the past and present. Limit your conversations; I can't stress this enough. Stop announcing your ideas and just make them happen. Everyone isn't rooting for you, so your best bet is to limit your future to only people who aren't offensive or irritated when you speak on them. Keep going no matter the circumstances; if you quit now, you'll never know what could possibly change your life. Once you learn your lesson, don't repeat the same mistake. Even if you don't feel like it, you are victorious. When it rains on a planted seed, eventually it produces fruit. Remember that anything is possible. ANYTHING. Know the difference between havoc and hope and remain hopeful that things will change. Set realistic goals for yourself and examine every so often to hold yourself accountable. Last, but not least, once the old has passed away, take a breather and embrace the new that has begun. So, I gave these tips to provide solutions for you to assess yourself during this phase and to prepare yourself for when the sun starts shining. I started this book largely as a way of finding answers for myself. My journey of self-discovery has helped me understand some important things more clearly, and I think that, if you're also stuck like I was, these lessons can help you move forward too. I can't wait for your struggle to turn into success.

With peace and love,

Shayla